The SHOUT

Finding the Prophetic Voice in Unexpected Places

Hannah Adair Bonner

The SHOUT

Finding the Prophetic Voice in Unexpected Places

"Shout loudly; don't hold back; raise your voice like a trumpet!"
—Isaiah 58:1

A Six-Week Study

The Shout
Finding the Prophetic Voice in Unexpected Places
by Hannah Adair Bonner
Copyright © 2016 by Abingdon Press
All rights reserved.

Scripture quotations in this publication, unless otherwise indicated, are from the Common English Bible, © Copyright 2011 by Common English Bible, and are used by permission.

Scripture quotations noted NRSV are taken from the New Revised Standard Version of the Bible, copyright 1989, Division of Christian Education of the National Council of the Churches of Christ in the United States of America. Used by permission. All rights reserved.

ISBN-13: 9781501816239

16 17 18 19 20 21 22 23 24 25—10 9 8 7 6 5 4 3 2 1

Manufactured in the United States of America

CONTENTS

Language is important. Words can either open doors or close them. Words can create space for creativity to flow, or they can leave us feeling boxed in and trapped. In a world so saturated with words, when new combinations are flowing through our social media feeds at a rate faster than we could ever think to consume them, few people take the time to savor and contemplate which words to use and how to order them. In fact, words are even starting to lose limbs from their body as "your" becomes "ur" to save characters, and "I don't know" becomes "idk." As we move increasingly into using codes of commonly used words and phrases, our sentences take on less beauty and creativity.

I speak of this dilemma not out of superior sanctity, but because it is my own experience. I mourn the loss of my vocabulary. I cherish books with paper pages as if they are sacred, yet the majority of the words I consume on a daily basis are hastily typed with thumbs and posted without thinking or editing. I devour them at a rate that leaves little opportunity for them to achieve permanence in the landscape of my mind.

Enter the poet. It is their duty, responsibility, and calling to cherish the word. They remind us that the thoughts in our minds, the emotions in our hearts, and the rationale behind our actions are often formed from words, and therefore they can be altered by words. By cradling the word and carefully deciding where to place it on the page, the work of the poet illustrates for us the power that words carry. There is a reason why Jesus was first described in John's Gospel as the Word made flesh. Bringing words to life has the power to change the world.

We can think of Scripture's prophets as spoken word poets. They brought the power of words to life in spoken performances to help their audience understand God and the divine vision for their world. The poet Isaiah had quite a gift for using words. It was a gift so profound that he imprinted his work not only into our sacred text, but into our collective reality. The words of Isaiah 58:6 (NRSV), "Is not this the fast that I choose: to loose the bonds of injustice," sound at least vaguely familiar to many people.

The importance of the spoken word piece found in Isaiah 58 is that it captures the frustration that many people feel when any religious movement becomes institutionalized and loses the heart of why it exists. In this passage, Isaiah describes a people who are, by their own standards, above reproach. They fast. They wear sackcloth and ashes, which is like donning black in mourning for their mistakes. They pray. Yet, they are frustrated because they feel like God is not paying attention to their cry.

Through Isaiah's spoken word, God responds very concisely with a challenging truth: It is the people themselves who are not listening, not paying attention to God, because they do not hear the cry of the needy. As God looks at the way they practice their religion, it looks like they are doing so in order to hurt rather than heal others. They fast and pray, certainly, but meanwhile, they fight; they oppress others; they strike others. Their religious rituals are of no use to God.

In Isaiah 58, God says do not focus on these rituals you pride yourself on carrying out. Instead, God says, if you want to make me happy, do what I asked you to do. Feed the hungry, clothe the naked, house the homeless, be forces of healing and restoration in your community.

Therefore, God instructs the prophet Isaiah, "Shout loudly; don't hold back; raise your voice like a trumpet!" (Isaiah 58:1). The prophet is to shout to God's people, announcing both their crimes and the life of justice God truly desires among them.

Thousands of years later, Isaiah's word still ring true. Why? Because people still create religious institutions that run the risk of forgetting their true purpose. Perhaps it is because we like to create God and our religions in our own image, imagining them to hate those we hate, love those we love, and silence those we silence. We do not want a movement that challenges us to change. Yet, without change, there is no movement, and without movement, there is only death.

And so, we Shout.

A month after the fatal shooting of Michael Brown in Ferguson, Missouri, The Shout community emerged in Houston, Texas, as a place to bring people together. We sought to understand and proclaim our identity as family and our responsibility to live as if the suffering of one is the responsibility of all. Each week, people throughout our community began to gather to Whisper, to talk about what was happening in the community, and to build relationships with one another. Once a month, that Whisper would build to a Shout where artists from throughout the community gathered at a large event to answer a compelling question, drawn from one of the directives of Isaiah 58. When the prophet lifted up "setting free the mistreated," we asked, "What is freedom?" When Isaiah called for "not hiding from your own family," we asked, "Who is your family?" And when Isaiah promised that justice would lead to healing and restoration, we asked, "How can we be whole?" The artists' responses to these questions are designed to provoke action. We call that action an Echo.

The SHOUT

The Shout is more than a mic; it's a movement. The goal of the Shout is the Echo—the action through which we pursue justice in our midst and lift up the needy, the hungry, the homeless, the mistreated, and the disrespected.

I am convinced that the prophetic Shout in today's world comes not from institutional leaders, but from within our communities, from artists and activists who feel God's frustration at the injustices that exists in our society. It is my hope and prayer that you will learn to hear the shout in your own community and to echo it with action, or perhaps with a shout of your own.

This book and the accompanying videos are meant to help you do that. You will hear the Shout coming out of Houston through the contributions of some of the Shout artists. You will be invited to understand their words through creative, artistic responses of your own: through drawing, writing, and poetry. You will Whisper together with other members of your small group each week. You will be encouraged to listen for the Shout in your own community, visiting new places to hear new voices. You will be called to Echo the shout with action, seeking justice for those around you.

Throughout this book you will have the opportunity to engage with some of the Shout artists through their written reflections or through videos. It could not be more fitting that the first poet you encounter would be one who was at the first Whisper, and who gave birth to a piece of the vision of the Shout when he spoke these words: "I don't want to preach to the choir. I don't want everyone in the room to merely be nodding their head in agreement." It was then that we discovered that gathering a diverse audience was just as important as gathering a diverse group of artists. For only together, artists and audience combined, will we be able to Echo. I leave you with this poem by Karega Ani and his powerful call to words that incite action.

Verb

What is a poem absent the context of motion
a meandering spark of nebulous intent
a senseless sentiment bereft of sphere
an ultimately monumental apparition
a lie of omission
and a trivial pursuit of nothing
there can be no intensity before breathing
before tasting the gun smoke
rebellion and anguish in the air
before inhaling the acrimonious stench
of one-sided comfortable silences
and before biting one's tongue until rage and red ink
suddenly crescendo into a scream

you're a poet...

so what?

a world full of torment and vitriolic laughter
is no place for empty sentiments
in the end what sacrament
will you have sacrificed silence for
what will be the punch line of it all
when the stars are obfuscated by
your failure to protect the sky
and all of the water is as black
as the hearts of the damned
and the Earth has chosen to mirror
the austerity of men
when all the choirs have died
and there's no one left to praise you
who will you pray to

who will be your refuge
when you finally deduce that you are small?

will you awaken
when the apocalypse descends
will your words miraculously echo new meaning
alighting seraphic wings to reach the ears of God
an apology shabbily prefacing their recollections
when there is nothing left to say

in real life
what do your insights incite
where is your wit
the incisive intent of your pen
what hours odds and ends are too long for your will
too over the top for your "god given gifts"
how will you be remembered

in the end
as you reached for the stars
how deep did you dig
were you the oracle that God intended
the deliverer of liberation
diminishing the sum of the dimness
if it took withholding nothing to save a no one
how much were you willing to give them
when it is all said and done
what truly was?
in retrospect
when you spoke
what did you move?
    –Karega Ani, Copyright 2015

WHERE IS JUSTICE?

"Isn't this the fast I choose: releasing wicked restraints, untying the ropes of a yoke, setting free the mistreated, and breaking every yoke?" (Isaiah 58:6).

Before we find the words, "Shout loudly; don't hold back; raise your voice like a trumpet!" in Isaiah 58, the same prophet writes these words from Isaiah 40:13-14: "Who directed the LORD's spirit and acted as God's advisor? Whom did he consult for enlightenment? Who taught him the path of justice and knowledge and explained to him the way of understanding?"

The questions are rhetorical, for the answer is, of course, no one. Justice, like knowledge and enlightenment, emerges from God. Justice is so central to the character of God, so embedded in the heart of God, so characteristic of the nature of God that we cannot orient our lives toward true justice without being oriented toward God. Likewise, we cannot be fully oriented toward God without pursuing justice. Perhaps that is why Proverbs 28:5 says, "Evil people don't understand justice, but those who seek the LORD understand everything."

When we consider the question, "What is justice," we must acknowledge that many, often competing definitions of justice exist in our world. For some, the word *justice* might conjure images of a judge and a legal system. Others might think of retribution or vengeance. Still other may imagine a police officer, and this image might make them feel safe or alarmed.

What does the word *justice* bring to mind for you? Write a brief word association poem to uncover what this word means to you. Supply a single word to fill in the blank, or experiment with different words that round out different aspects of justice.

Justice is _____

Take a moment and compare your responses with others in your group. Do you all seem to have the same understanding of justice, or do responses vary? Why is justice such a complex concept in our world?

Scriptural justice is much more than a theory, a topic, or a system. As it is described in the Prophets and the Psalms, justice is a whole lifestyle, a distinct orientation toward other people, especially the socially vulnerable. Prophets like Isaiah recognized the ongoing oppression of widows, orphans, foreigners, and other marginalized classes of people. They spoke out against attitudes and practices that regarded these persons as less-than-human, which enabled others to take advantage of them. God's justice, they said, went against such oppression, taking special concern to lift up these vulnerable people. At its root, justice involves the *humanization* of other people, regarding them as fellow human beings and ensuring the fair treatment of all (From "Justice, OT," by Harold V. Bennett in *The New Interpreter's Dictionary of the Bible*, Volume 3 [Abingdon Press, 2008]; pages 476–477).

> "Lord, to those who hunger, give bread. And to those who have bread, give a hunger for justice."—Latin American prayer

The prophets lift up this vision of justice as God's desire for their world. We can understand justice, then, as a way of worshiping God by striving for a world that reflects God's character. It's an attitude that affects our relationships with others and the paths we follow in life. Justice is not a destination. It's not a place or a set of circumstances to which we can point and say that we have achieved it. Justice is, in fact, an ever-unfolding, lifelong journey, and it cannot be undertaken in seclusion. Justice lies in the merging of stories, the collision between hearts and truth, the opening of eyes and ears and hands.

When I lived in the Isaiah House, an intentional Christian community in Durham, North Carolina, there was a woman across the street who sought to create this type of justice on her front porch. She painted a sign on a piece of wood that said, "Uplift East Durham," and she invited people from throughout the community to come and talk about what that meant to them. East Durham was an impoverished area of town, and one thing that concerned the residents was a plan to widen the two-lane road that ran through our neighborhood into a busy highway. At face value, many people in Durham would have seen this as an improvement because it would make their lives easier. They would be able to pass through our neighborhood without having to slow down. For the residents, however, there would be a

> "If you have come here to help me, you are wasting your time. But if you have come because your liberation is bound up with mine, then let us work together."— Aboriginal Activists, 1970's

cost. It would cost them the destruction of the only grocery store that was willing to operate in that part of the city. It would cost them the historic church building that was a foundation of the community. It would make life in the neighborhood much more dangerous for their children, as well as for the largely pedestrian population that would have to walk across that busy road to get to work. It would make it possible for people from outside of town to speed through our neighborhood and into our city without having to look us in the eyes. It would weaken the community that was already struggling. The question then became, should our impoverished neighborhood have to lose its access to fresh food, a place of worship, and a sense of safety and dignity in order that people from outside the community could drive through it more quickly? So the folks on the porch organized in order to ask the Mayor: Where is justice? For them, justice meant lifting up East Durham, ensuring that the city would care for them as its people.

Draw a picture of what you imagine this neighborhood might look like and what would change if the road were widened.

"If you're born with a silver spoon in your mouth. If you are born on food stamps. In the ghetto or in the suburbs or in the projects or in the palace. If justice is where you're headed, then you'll always end up headed in the same direction. It'll pull us like the North Star. It guides your actions.... So where is justice? It's somewhere we can walk together. Hopefully, someday, someone will live in that place called Justice; and the next generation will live in a place called Peace."
—Noah Rattler

As you draw, consider the following questions, then discuss them with your group:

What signifies injustice in your drawing?

What signs of hope for justice do you see?

Consider your own community and your place within it. Do you identify more with the residents of this East Durham neighborhood, or with those who might wish to drive through it more quickly?

What will it mean for you to pursue justice in your own community?

The people gathered on the front porch around the Uplift East Durham sign made justice physical. It was something tangible that they sought, with real consequences in their community. They used their feet, their voices, their minds, and their energy to articulate what justice looked like and felt like for them.

Watch the poem that Jeremyah and Nyne performed in honor of their friend Sandra Bland. Sandra was someone they knew from college who had come back to their alma mater, Prairie View A&M University, to interview for a job. She had just gotten the job at the HBU (Historically Black University) when she was pulled over as she left campus for not using her turn signal. The traffic stop was escalated by the officer, according to the Department of Public Safety, and he ended up trying to pull her from her car before threatening her with his Taser and leading her out of the line of sight of cameras. She was arrested in a rough manner, and three days later she was found dead in her jail cell. They said she hung herself, but people like Jeremyah began to ask: "What happened to Sandra Bland?"

How did Jeremyah and Nyne use the gifts that they had to articulate what justice is?

Scriptural justice is a physical thing. It is about the way that we exist in this world. It is not only about how we think, but what we do and say. To be sure, justice can find itself in books and dialogues and lectures, but it is never content in those places. Justice is always restless, seeking to break out of the hypothetical and take on flesh and walk around. It is beating in the heart of its Creator, and like its Creator it will not be content until it has been made flesh.

It is made flesh in you and in me.

Justice is made flesh in muscles that have relaxed instead of tensed in their seats when sitting at the table of struggle; because even when discussions become uncomfortable, we have no plans to get up and leave.

Justice is made flesh in ears willing to hear things that make us uncomfortable. It's made flesh when we ask, "What if this is true?" even when it means changing the way we look at our own actions or those of our family.

Justice is made flesh in eyes that examine not only how events impact ourselves, but how they impact those around us.

Justice is made flesh in feet that are willing to step out in solidarity with those who are suffering, which keep walking in the conviction that none of us will know justice until we all know justice.

Justice is made flesh in hands that are willing to release their "more than enough" so that others may simply have "enough."

Look up and read Maya Angelou's poem, "Still I Rise" (you can find it online at *www.poets.org/poetsorg/poem/still-i-rise,* or search for it elsewhere on the Internet). After you read it, compare it with your word association poem on page 14. Consider the following questions:

Where are there commonalities between your poem and "Still I Rise?"

Where can you see that your perspectives differ from those of Maya Angelou as expressed in her poem? What can you learn from these differences?

What seems to be Maya Angelou's vision of justice? How do you think she would answer the question, "Where is justice?"

Though it doesn't actually use the English word *justice*, Isaiah 58 paints a clear picture of scriptural justice, as well as what injustice looks like among the people of Judah during Isaiah's time. Read through the entire chapter, and underline words that are repeated or that stand out to you.

Isaiah 58

[1] Shout loudly; don't hold back;
  raise your voice like a trumpet!
Announce to my people their crime,
  to the house of Jacob their sins.
[2] They seek me day after day,
  desiring knowledge of my ways
  like a nation that acted righteously,
  that didn't abandon their God.
They ask me for righteous judgments,
  wanting to be close to God.
[3] "Why do we fast and you don't see;
  why afflict ourselves and you don't notice?"
Yet on your fast day you do whatever you want,
  and oppress all your workers.
[4] You quarrel and brawl, and then you fast;
  you hit each other violently with your fists.
You shouldn't fast as you are doing today
  if you want to make your voice heard on high.
[5] Is this the kind of fast I choose,
  a day of self-affliction,
  of bending one's head like a reed
  and of lying down in mourning clothing and ashes?
  Is this what you call a fast,
    a day acceptable to the Lord?
[6] Isn't this the fast I choose:
  releasing wicked restraints, untying the ropes of a yoke,
  setting free the mistreated,
  and breaking every yoke?
[7] Isn't it sharing your bread with the hungry
  and bringing the homeless poor into your house,
  covering the naked when you see them,
  and not hiding from your own family?
[8] Then your light will break out like the dawn,
  and you will be healed quickly.
Your own righteousness will walk before you,
  and the Lord's glory will be your rear guard.

[9] Then you will call, and the LORD will answer;
you will cry for help, and God will say, "I'm here."
If you remove the yoke from among you,
the finger-pointing, the wicked speech;
[10] if you open your heart to the hungry,
and provide abundantly for those who are afflicted,
your light will shine in the darkness,
and your gloom will be like the noon.
[11] The LORD will guide you continually
and provide for you, even in parched places.
He will rescue your bones.
You will be like a watered garden,
like a spring of water that won't run dry.
[12] They will rebuild ancient ruins on your account;
the foundations of generations past you will restore.
You will be called Mender of Broken Walls,
Restorer of Livable Streets.
[13] If you stop trampling the Sabbath,
stop doing whatever you want on my holy day,
and consider the Sabbath a delight,
sacred to the LORD, honored,
and honor it instead of doing things your way,
seeking what you want and doing business as usual,
[14] then you will take delight in the LORD.
I will let you ride on the heights of the earth;
I will sustain you with the heritage of your ancestor Jacob.
The mouth of the LORD has spoken.

"Justice is treating others and yourself with the understanding that what's equal isn't always fair and what's fair isn't always equal. (I think specifically of laws created to help or aid those with disabilities etc.)"—Jasminne Mendez, poet

Are the words you underlined words that you hear on a regular basis? If you use social media a great deal, try searching for some of them on social media, using hashtags such as #righteousness or even simple searches on the web. Search also for #justice and

#injustice, as well as synonyms such as #healing or #oppression. Try to gather a clear picture of what these words and concepts mean in our online world, which provides a window into people's lives and experiences.

What are people saying? Sift past the misuses of the words—for instance, having to eat one percent Greek yogurt instead of zero percent Greek yogurt is not #thestruggleisreal, and getting a dirty look when you catcall a woman is not #injustice. What remains and stands out to you as important? Is there anything happening that you were not aware of, or that you were not aware impacted people strongly?

"Justice is the outcome of integral action; the uncompromised manifestation of good."—Corinna Delgado, poet

How do these insights from social media challenge your own understanding of justice?

Justice is a journey, but we can only find our way together. The Wesleyan tradition of Christianity teaches that we find our way with Scripture interpreted through tradition, reason, and experience. This approach recognizes that the Bible is not a universal answer-book or a static, comprehensive authority on all matters of life. Our traditions as people of faith, our intellectual capacity for reason, and our experiences of God are all gifts that God has given to help us understand God's living word and how it influences our lives today.

"Justice is the road on which we travel together, listening to each other, protecting each other from insecurity and caring for each other's well-being. It is not a destination, it is a path, a Way of living together."
—Noah Rattler, philosopher

DELICIA ARRIOLA, "THE DREAM"

Delicia Arriola is a native Houstonian and graduate of Jarvis Christian College. After college, she began her career as an education specialist and served as the liaison for the Young Urban Professionals branch of the Houston Urban League. She has worked as a senior training manager, a pre-K teacher, and a dental sales representative. Her eclectic background and wealth of knowledge motived her to leave the corporate world and peruse her passion in the hair care industry and in performing arts. Delicia is the owner of Runway Salon and is currently working as a stylist with a holistic approach to healthy hair care. She is also pursuing her passion and love of the arts as a poet, actor, writer, visual artist, and public speaker. Delicia has hit the poetry stages as "The Dream" with a powerful voice that captivates audiences and tackles many relevant topics, including social justice. She has used the Shout stage as a platform to be heard, to create awareness and lend a voice to the community she is a part of. Her purpose is to bring awareness, inspire, cultivate, and motivate people to embrace their full potential and follow their dreams.

In each era, we have different struggles and opportunities. We therefore have different experiences and understandings of the world that we bring to our application and interpretation of Scripture. In many faith traditions, the voices of women have been marginalized in the past, but are now receiving renewed appreciation and value in the conversation about how to live out Scripture. Though many of us do not remember a time when women couldn't teach and preach, this is in fact a relatively new development in the history of Christianity. In addition, we increasingly live in a global world, where perspectives and relationships transcend geographical boundaries. We can hold conversations not just with people in our neighborhoods, but with people from all over the world. This makes it possible to hear perspectives on Scripture that come from the widest possible spectrum of experiences throughout the world.

Our collective experience of God is incredibly diverse and nuanced, and we have more opportunities than ever before to share our experiences and to understand the experiences of others. What an exciting time to be alive! So many different experiences of God's grace can be a wonderful gift to help us understand God's word through the Scriptures. How then can we afford to miss opportunities to hear from as much of our community as possible?

> "Justice is in the scales but rather if the tilt is fair is up to circumstance."
> —Ahmad Hygh, poet

If we are to understand Scriptures about justice and injustice through experience, what experience do we have with justice? Have we ourselves experienced injustice? If we have a hard time answering that, then it is probably time to listen to someone who has experienced injustice. After all, the best person to describe what an apple tastes like is a person who has actually eaten one.

What experience do you have with justice and injustice?

Who should you be listening to in your community?

Who has a different, perhaps better, experience of justice and injustice than you do?

DONALD COLLINS

Donald Collins is a Houston-based artist who works in a variety of mediums. He sees life as a canvas and tries to stay in creative mode as much as possible, finding inspiration everywhere he looks. He sees himself first and foremost as a quick sketch artist, and he pursues this medium with pen, ink, and passion. It is a way of remaining grounded and maintaining connection with the world around him. He paints as a release of memories and dreams, exploring the inner world with which he constructs his view of the outer world. Donald is a social activist who uses his art as a medium for change. He seeks to bring the viewer to see the world from a different perspective

There comes a point at which our experience—or another's experience—shows us something different in the Scriptures than what we see through tradition or reason. Those who have contributed to Christian tradition often had limited experiences of their own. Take, for example, the words of some early church fathers on a woman's place. Many of them went seemingly out of their way to justify the passages in Scripture where women are forbidden to teach, providing all sorts of reasons why women are inferior to men and therefore prohibited from instructing them (see 1 Corinthians 14:34 and 1 Timothy 2:12).

Some of their arguments are downright silly. And yet as ludicrous as they may sound to us, they come from the same people who wrote much of what we call tradition. So, when some of the things they say in tradition conflict with the experience of some women today, we take it to the Lord and seek to discern what lines up with the God of justice and love. We ask ourselves, is this the way that Jesus treated and spoke to women?

We take our minds and hearts and even our Scripture and tradition with us when God says, "Wash yourselves; make yourselves clean; remove the evil of your doings from before my eyes; cease to do evil, learn to do good; seek justice, rescue the oppressed, defend the orphan, plead for the widow" (Isaiah 1:16-17, NRSV).

In a way, we must create justice even with a Scripture and Tradition that have been used in very unjust ways: the rationalization of slavery, the silencing of women, the slaughter of indigenous peoples, and the rejection of LGBTQ teens from their parents' homes. Throughout all those years, members within each of those groups of people have been able to pick up the Bible, wash it from the evil with which it has been burdened, and find in it their justice and liberation.

NOAH RATTLER

A native of the Crestmont Park Subdivision in Houston, Texas, Noah Rattler holds a bachelor of science in mechanical engineering and physics from Prairie View A&M University. While finishing his formal education, Noah decided to dedicate his time to his community. In 2005, he started volunteering with the homeless at Houston's SEARCH Project in an effort to understand the complex interaction between the many forces that contribute to homelessness today. In 2007, as part of an effort to raise awareness for the homeless situation in the United States, he went on an eighteen-hundred-mile walk from Houston, Texas, to the Pacific Ocean at Santa Monica, California, with the help of Congresswoman Sheila Jackson Lee. In 2008, as a follow-up to the walk, he initiated SleepOut Saturday, an event that gives participants a behind-the-scenes look at homelessness from several perspectives.

Those voices continue to speak today not only from our pulpits but also from our streets. It is imperative for us to listen carefully so that we might hear voices in our community. At times it can feel overwhelming because there are so many people struggling with so many different injustices. Often it feels like the whole world must change at once. At other times, it can feel bewildering not to know how to engage, or how to stand in solidarity. And sometimes, when we experience injustice ourselves, it can be so tiring to try to explain to people what is happening and why they should care when we ourselves are just trying to survive.

Pause. Take a deep breath. Say these words from Psalm 46:10 (NRSV), taking a deep breath at the end of each line.

Be still
And know
That I
Am God

Every journey begins with a first step. What will yours be? What might be taking place in your community? Where is the front porch in your community where people are gathering?

Consider the video from the poet The Dream. She is very specific and intentional about her location. A couple months after Jeremyah and Nyne performed their piece, she performed hers about Sandra Bland in front of the Department of Public Safety where Lutherans, Presbyterians, and United Methodists had gathered that day to demand accountability for the man who had arrested Sandra. The Dream had an investment in getting answers; she had a child who was a student at the school where Sandra was arrested. She made her cry heard in an intentional location.

Where is the prophetic cry being made public through art? In the graffiti on the bridge? In the slam poetry competition at the coffee shop? Where is it that you need to have eyes to see and ears to hear, not in order to approach someone else's experience as a consumer, but in order to respond? (Although let us be clear, consuming prophetic art through purchasing it is a way of investing in prophetic work in your community and magnifying its power. Supporting artists is itself a form of justice.)

Here are the words of one poet in our Shout community, Cara Gee, who you may not find in a church, but who has a lot to say to the church about how we can be just:

> As a very young teen, I experienced unspeakable violence at the church I grew up in. Through being sexually assaulted by a church deacon, I was transformed from innocent to cynical in approximately fifteen minutes. I later sought counsel from my youth pastor and was informed that my rapist was "clearly fighting a spiritual battle." That was it. No further action taken. No justice. No peace, only bitterness and anger. I lost all belief in the Church as a whole, in God, in people.
>
> As an adult, I have struggled with the idea of "finding justice." In the journey, I've found that my sense of closure has to come from doing my own work—from building community in solidarity with people I can consider my allies. That is my justice. It comes from being heard, believed, and loved in the heartache. To be just is to bear witness, no matter how difficult or painful, to the experiences of others. It comes from a place of radical love, and is not just an act of benevolence. I would even go so far as to say that justice is not an act. It is a state of being interconnected with those around you— validating their experiences and lifting them up when they cannot carry the load alone.
>
> Healing is found where there is justice. Justice is found wherever there is a wound being bandaged by willing hands.

Is there a prophetic shout within you that your congregation or community needs to hear? Is there something that troubles you that must be spoken, or written, or drawn? Is there something inside of you that must come out? Justice is restless. It cannot be contained.

"Isn't it...not hiding from your own family?" (Isaiah 58:7)

WHO IS YOUR FAMILY?

Family. That word has different connotations for all of us. For some people it evokes feelings of warmth and safety, but for others it raises images of danger and abuse. Some people hold tight to a sense of "family honor," which they will die to defend because it is central to their identity. Others feel that they are responsible only for their own actions and legacy, and family plays little role in who they know themselves to be.

Regardless of how we understand or experience family, the notion of family that Jesus presents through his words and actions is something altogether revolutionary. The family Jesus lifts up involves commitment and sacrifice, and it is built on a relationship that transcends blood kinship. God stands at its center.

In Matthew 12:46-50, a passage that makes many mothers wince, Christ redefines family as those who seek righteousness:

[46] While Jesus was speaking to the crowds, his mother and his brothers stood outside trying to speak with him.
[47] Someone said to him, "Look, your mother and brothers are outside wanting to speak with you."

[48] Jesus replied, "Who is my mother? Who are my brothers?"
[49] He stretched out his hand toward his disciples and said, "Look, her are my mother and my brothers. [50] Whoever does the will of my Father who is in heaven is my brother, sister, and mother."

The SHOUT

"Love is neither sentimental nor a passing emotion. It is the recognition of a covenant, of mutual belonging. It is listening to others, being concerned for them and feeling empathy... It is to see their beauty and to reveal it to them."—Jean Vanier, *Community and Growth*

Readers often miss the radical repercussions of Jesus' words here. He actually transformed what it means to be family in a time when family was central to life and society. This simple but challenging statement was one of the most countercultural things that Jesus did. Like his liberating attitude towards women, the implications of his words are not always put into action. Yet if we even stop to consider the beginning of the Lord's Prayer, we can see just how central this notion of family should be to Christian life. The Lord's Prayer begins with the words, "Our Father..." (see Matthew 6:9-13).

Many Christians recite this prayer regularly, and we often do a lot of talking about the meaning of the word *father* or, as some might prefer to translate it, "parent." But how much do we think about that first word, *our*? To me that is the more significant word for us in today's world. What, or more importantly, *who* do we mean when we say "our"? If God is our parent, who are our sisters and brothers? Who is alongside us as we raise our prayer?

Who do we mean when we say "our"? Take some time to make a list of who comes to mind when you say "our."

Look back over your list, and ask yourself the following questions:

Who is missing? Who do I need to carry into prayer with me?

What might I be missing because I do not join my prayer with theirs?

When Isaiah raises his voice like a trumpet (Isaiah 58:1), he reminds God's people of the critical need to care for their kinsfolk. "Isn't this the fast I choose," the prophet asks, then names various acts of justice as the lifestyle that will result in God's blessing. He concludes his list with "not hiding from your own family" (Isaiah 58:6-7). It's no coincidence that an appeal to family drives Isaiah's point home. The people must assist and lift up their own flesh and blood. Whether one's neighbors are poor, or homeless, or hungry, or naked matters not; the issue is settled with their identification as "family." The people's kinship with one another trumps distinctions rooted in class or circumstance.

When we couple Isaiah's exhortation with Jesus' understanding of family, we arrive at some life-changing implications for how we relate to the world. If we saw all the people that God claims as children as our own kin, such a view would bring about a revolution in the way we treat others. It could even have the power to change the world.

When Michael Brown was shot on August 9, 2014, the implications of that event quickly became apparent. People all around the nation were in intense mourning, and many of them were furious. It felt intolerable to them that another young black man had lost his life. They mourned as if he were family, as if he were their own brother. The thing about family is this: It doesn't matter how or why a family member dies. When family dies, you mourn.

For much of the nation, however, people wanted answers so they could decide whether Michael had "deserved" to die. They wanted to know if he had committed a crime.

The reality, however, is that when family dies, we mourn. Unfortunately, it seemed that those who mourned and those who said they needed more information to decide on a response often broke down along racial/ethnic lines. To put it bluntly, people who were white like me were having a hard time mourning Michael Brown.

Why do you think people respond differently if the person suffering looks like them? How do you think God feels about that? Draw a picture of what God's family photo would look like.

As my community struggled with how to approach this tragedy, a memory came to me of a child I had lived with during my days at the Isaiah House. One sunny day, I sat in the backyard with this young, African American boy who was about six years old and wearing a red T-shirt. His family had moved in after they were evicted from a house down the street.

In his lap, the boy held a young baby. The infant was Caucasian according to society's categories, but he was human by birth and God's by baptism.

We sat in the hammock under the pecan tree and swayed, as the young boy held the baby in his lap. He played games with the baby's fingers and made him laugh, each one of them delighting in the other. Sunlight fell on us through the leaves overhead, warming our faces and hearts.

Finally, the young boy turned to me and said, referring to the baby, "God loves him, right?"

"Yes," I said with a slight smile.

Then after a pause, he said, "And God loves me."

"Yes," I said.

"And I love the baby." Another pause. I was not quite sure what he was getting at.

Then he concluded triumphantly, "I think that's what Martin Luther King, Jr. was talking about."

His wisdom left me in amazement. He had been learning about Martin Luther King, Jr.

> "We are one in the Spirit, we are one in the Lord..."
> —Peter Scholtes

in school and was wise enough to realize that there was something important and revolutionary about his love. By welcoming that baby into the family of God, he recognized that choice would have an impact on both their lives. He realized that the responsibility they had to each other had the power to change the world if they lived it out well.

"I think you're right," I answered, putting my arm around him.

Can it really be as simple as that? Is it so simple that a child can easily understand it, even though adults spend their whole lives rejecting it?

In honor of that young boy, in September of 2014, the month after Michael Brown's death, we asked our first question at The Shout: Who is your family? Poets from throughout Houston came together with one goal in mind: to help the people in the room claim one another as family.

This was no small task, and it remains unfinished. Claiming someone else as family is not an easy thing for everyone to do, and it should never be forced or demanded. The invitation to become family can only be offered as a hand outstretched to see if anyone will step out and grab it.

When artists open the depths of their heart and emotions to an audience, they make that invitation to connect with their story and be changed by it—if the audience members are bold enough. Inherent to the invitation, however, is responsibility. If we accept our identity as family, then we have a responsibility to do something about that relationship.

Take the performance from Dulcie Veluthukaran, for instance. If this were an invitation from her to connect as family, what responsibility would come with it? What action would be required if you were to accept an identity that is united to hers as family?

DULCIE "DIGH" VELUTHUKARAN

Dulcie "Digh" Veluthukaran is a singer-songwriter, poet, and teacher. She has served as a coach for Houston's youth slam team, Meta-Four Houston, and is an active member of the Houston VIP slam team. A 2008 Teach For America alumn, Digh currently serves as an English teacher at Alexander Hamilton Middle School. She holds a master of arts in English and creative writing.

Often, we take family relationships with the world around us lightly. We seek the benefits without the sacrifices. We want to go on mission trips to Guatemala and take pictures hugging children…but then what do we do when those same children cross our borders seeking safety? Do we seek them out and embrace them then? Are they still our family? When we truly regard others as family, we recognize that they make a claim on our lives the same as we make on theirs.

If we see one another as family, then suffering within the family will become intolerable to us. It will become difficult to enjoy the comfort of our lives if our family members are suffering. Sacrificing to bring them justice will not be a difficult choice. It will feel—and really be—natural to protect one another, to fight for one another, to dream with one another.

AHMAD HYGH, "NYNE"

Nyne The Poet was born and raised in Houston, Texas. Nyne is one of the premier poets from the Houston area and has been doing poetry for twelve years. Nyne is a one-time National Poetry Slam Group Piece champion. He is also a college Poetry Slam semifinalist. Nyne teaches poetry to high school students and also does charity work with The Shout.

Here are the words of one poet in our Shout community whom you may not find in a church, but who has a lot to say to the church about how we can be just. Ahmad Hygh, known as the poet Nyne, reflects on what it means to live as family with people who are not related to you by blood:

To me, while you have got blood relatives that are your family, family also extends past those borders. I grew up in a single parent home with just my mother; so my father figures, I had to handpick them. My uncles, I handpicked them. My aunties, I handpicked them. So to help you identify who your family is, I'm going to give you a couple pointers from what I've learned.

1. Family keeps you out of trouble: My grandmother always told me that you know who your real family is if they can get you out of jail. Now in life, I've never gotten anyone out of jail physically. But I've convinced some people that what they were doing was not what they should be doing, or they were going to end up in jail.

2. Family prioritizes you over money: People will want to be your best friend, your brother, your sister, you auntie, your uncle, your cousin, your boo thang, over money and recognition and notoriety and power. Your real family—none of that matters. When I was traveling from Boston, my wallet was stolen and I couldn't get home. My Brother, Jeremyah, realized that I was gone from my daughter, and he didn't want the father of his goddaughter to be gone for that long, so he fronted me the plane ticket back home. He hasn't ever brought that money up, no matter how angry he gets at me, because we are family.

3. Family can disagree and stick together: Everyone varies in how they believe. The point of the matter is that you are

still family. They are still going to ride with you one hundred percent. That is the problem these days, when we disagree with someone, we don't want to talk anymore. Wiley might not believe in gay marriage, so Zachary called him a bigot; but Zachary don't believe in dating outside your race, so Wiley called him a racist. Because of that the two don't see each other, don't talk to each other. We have to see past that. We may not be the same, but that does not mean we are not family.

4. Family is recognized in the spirit: Something in your spirit is going to recognize each other. When you really start finding and recognizing who your real family is, who your brothers and sisters are who will ride for you, you got to make sure your spirit is in line. You know, a preacher and a cynic can be best friends. They can consider themselves brothers and sisters, two completely different paths through two completely different things, but their spirits are going to be what keeps them together.

5. Family respects you: Your blood family may disrespect you, they may not treat you like an important entity. Yet, in this world, you have to find people who respect you. It has to happen. Family is a frail but strong type of thing. That is why they call it a family tree. It starts small, it starts real delicate, but it can grow to be something strong and amazing and unmovable and solid. The branches can grow long and they can be full of leaves, or the tree can die immediately. Your real family just wants to be with you. Just so they can lift you up.

According to Nyne's checklist, who do you think in your town or city would see you as family?

Are there ways you could do a better job of being family to your community?

Part of what The Shout has striven to do is to help people to be better family to one another through understanding each other's lives. When we do that, we begin to do better at the scriptural exhortation to rejoice with those who rejoice and mourn with those who mourn (Romans 12:15). We begin to act more like family, and people recognize us as such.

OUTSPOKEN BEAN

Emanuelee "Outspoken Bean" is a performance poet, writer, compassionate mentor, electric entertainer, and an educator who calls San Antonio, Texas home. Bean travels the country performing his original works and inspiring creative minds. That work has taken him from Trinidad to Off-Broadway New York City and across the Houston Metropolitan area, where he inspires people from all walks of life to find their voice. A Texas Poet Laureate nominee, Bean has performed spoken word poetry since 2005. Since that time, he has ranked highly at the Individual World Poetry Slam, Group Piece Finals, and National Poetry Slam. In his senior year at Prairie View A&M University, Bean founded and coached the University's first poetry slam team. He serves as the Project Coordinator, Lead Coach, and mentor for Meta-Four Houston, where professional performance/slam poets encourage self-expression and literacy among Houston's youth through creative writing and performance. Check out his website, *www.outspokenbeanpoetry.com*.

In Outspoken Bean's performance he says, "We are a people who mourn." But whom do you mourn for?

Who is your family?

WHAT IS FREEDOM?

"Isn't this the fast I choose... setting free the mistreated..." (Isaiah 58:6).

Isaiah writes about the need for freedom among the people of Judah, saying that "setting free the mistreated" is integral to a fast that God will find acceptable (Isaiah 58:6). But what is freedom?

Several years ago, I spent time living at the Bahamas Methodist Habitat on an island named Eleuthera, which comes from the Greek word for "free" or "freedom." There are two stories that can be told about that island and how it received its name. The more predominant story goes as follows: In the late 1640's a group of English Puritans set out from Bermuda, where they lived, on a journey to resettle in the Bahamas where they could worship and practice their religion freely and without opposition. They called themselves the Eleutheran Adventurers. As they passed by a long island, one hundred miles long by two miles wide, they were caught in a storm and crashed into the Devil's Backbone, a tremendous underwater rock formation off the coast of the island. The survivors of the shipwreck made it to shore and found shelter in a large cathedral-like cave, which they later named Preacher's Cave. It was there, in that perfectly contoured space, that they gave thanks to God for their lives and celebrated their first worship service. Finding the island uninhabited, they settled there and continued to hold worship services in Preacher's Cave for the next one hundered years. That story is the one most commonly told about the island, because those with the pen in their hand tell the story from their perspective.

There is another story, however, about that island's discovery. The second story will tell you that the Eleutheran Adventurers found the beautiful island to be uninhabited not because it had gone undiscovered, but precisely because it had been discovered. This island was one of many whose population had been drained and decimated by Spanish explorers that arrived there in the early 1500's. The original Arawak inhabitants, the Lucayans, had been taken from the island to work the mines in Cuba and Hispaniola. This was in an era before the attention of European "explorers" had turned away from native populations and towards the continent of Africa to satiate their thirst for slaves. The uninhabited island that meant freedom for the Eleutheran Adventurers had been made possible by the enslavement and eventual destruction of an entire people.

> "Won't you help to sing, these songs of freedom?" — Bob Marley

Freedom is complicated. Isaiah speaks very clearly of freedom for "the mistreated" or, in the NRSV translation, "the oppressed" (Isaiah 58:6). But oppression has many faces. What looks like freedom for one person might turn out to be the same story of mistreatment and abuse for someone else. In seeking our own freedom, we must also be aware of the needs that others have. In striving for our own liberty, we must be careful that we do not jeopardize the liberty or well-being of another.

Freedom is something that we value and pursue, especially in our nation that we call the "Land of the Free." But the fact is that freedom doesn't mean the same thing to all of us. When Francis Scott Key first penned those lines about "the land of the free and the home of the brave" in 1814, many of our brothers and sisters were still held in the chains of slavery. America was no land of freedom for them. Humans always have a knack for applying concepts selectively, and those who have the power get to write the story from their perspective. We might also consider discussions about religious freedoms in our country in recent years. What some see as personal liberation others call oppression, and vice versa. Freedom is complicated. We do not all agree on what it is.

KAREGA ANI

Karega Ani is a performance poet and music producer from Houston, Texas. A one-time student of the legendary Ntozake Shange, he has been refining his unique literary and performance style for nearly twenty years, living by the credo that diligent preparation must always precede presentation. He is currently completing his master's degree in social justice at Marygrove College (Detroit, Michigan), as well as his debut anthology, *Wailing*.

In Karega Ani's piece on "What is freedom," he takes the listener on a journey through the process of African Americans finding liberty. What is it, ultimately, that he describes as the door to freedom? What is it that people need to be freed from? After watching his performance, consider how you would respond to him.

> "I have no ambition for power, and so with complete freedom, I tell the powerful what is good and what is bad."—Oscar Romero

What do we need to be freed from? Take some time and find a photo that represents what we as a society or a culture need to be set free from. Search for one online, choose one you have taken previously, or take a new one right now. Share your photo on social media with the hashtag #ShoutWhatIsFreedom, then spend some time looking through photos that others have shared. How do these photos help you answer the question, "What is freedom?"

Your photo will likely be different, perhaps very different, from the photos that other people take, because freedom means different things to different people. For instance, the ability to travel internationally is a freedom that many of us take for granted. For a young, white American, traveling to a new place—going to Guatemala to climb mountains, for instance—can be an expression and celebration of freedom. But we must consider that we don't expect this freedom to go both ways. We believe that people from Guatemala can't travel to our communities to climb mountains if they don't have the wealth and resources to obtain what we call legal immigration. The same young people that many of us rush to take pictures with on mission trips become criminals when they come to our country by the only means they can. This sobering fact illustrates the differing ideas we have about our own freedom and the freedom of others.

Does God distribute freedom equally at birth? What happens after birth or before birth that gives some of us more freedom and opportunities than others? How does God feel about this? In the space provided, write a short story in response to these questions.

The SHOUT

The Freedom of Humans and the Freedom of God

The freedom of humans and governments is not the same thing as the freedom of God, the freedom that Christ has given us. At times they overlap, and at times they conflict with one another. When they are in conflict, the people of God must speak up and act. In his *Letter From a Birmingham Jail*, King encouraged Christian leaders to use the freedom that Christ had given them to stand up against fear and speak out against racism and oppression. Our laws are meant to protect our freedom, but at times they do not safeguard everyone's freedom. When that happens, we must speak up until they ensure freedom for all. During the Civil Rights Movement, white leaders in the United States could live in safety and freedom if they kept their mouths shut about racism and segregation. But this was a false freedom, for it did not include all of God's family. Those who sought the true freedom of God had a responsibility to speak out against human laws that ensured freedom for some at the expense of others.

Paul's Letter to the Galatians can help us to see what true freedom must accomplish: "You were called to freedom, brothers and sisters; only don't let this freedom be an opportunity to indulge your selfish impulses, but serve each other through love" (Galatians 5:13). Paul speaks of the freedom that Christ has given those who follow him. This freedom is a great gift, but we are responsible for how we use it. Will we use it to set free the mistreated, as Isaiah says, working to ensure that they are not oppressed?

We are responsible for whether we use our freedom to harm or to help others. We do not need to feel guilt and shame if we have more freedom than someone else. What we do need to do is understand that if God desires us to set the oppressed free, then we have a responsibility to take strong and determined action if freedom is not extended to everyone. Lay aside guilt and pick up responsibility. Guilt paralyzes, but responsibility galvanizes.

To Be Set Free

In Joshua Hundl's Shout reflection, he shares some of his own story and struggle, particularly his struggle to hear God's voice. Look within yourself. How do you struggle to hear God's voice? How have you let other voices distract you from God's purpose and love for you? What lies do you need to lay aside in order to embrace God's freedom? Create an image of how it would feel to be set free.

JOSHUA HUNDL

Joshua Hundl is currently in his final year of the Creative Writing program at the University of Houston. In that time, he's written two short films and several plays that have been produced (as well as many that have not). He's been published in Glass Mountain, spoken many times for The Shout (a Houston-based poetry/spoken-word movement), and he is currently finishing the script for his latest play, *Cross Talk*.

The SHOUT

For me, the lie that I had listened to my whole life was that I could not be and should not be a leader in the church because I was a woman. I had allowed passages like 1 Corinthians 14:34-36, which says that women should be silent in church, to silence me. It took intervention directly from the Holy Spirit before I was willing to let go of that lie. One day, while studying that Scripture, I narrowed in on the rebuke at the end of that passage: "Did the word of God originate with you?" I quickly realized that there were two meanings for the phrase "the word of God": It could refer to the gospel message or to the Word made flesh, which is Jesus Christ. I discovered also that there were a couple of possible translations for the verb *originate*, including "to be spoken or proclaimed" and "to be born or descended from someone." Matching it up, I realized that it was a woman who first spoke the gospel message that Jesus had risen from the dead, and it was a woman who had first given birth to the Word made flesh, Jesus Christ. It was as if God was saying to me, "How many possible meanings of this statement do I have to offer before it loses its power to condemn you? When will you see that I said to the women at the tomb 'Go and tell'?" Looking up from my Bible in the library that day, I just kept saying to myself, "I'm free. I'm free." After years of being oppressed as a woman, I experienced freedom by the Holy Spirit through the very Scripture that had condemned me.

God does not wish us only to find freedom for ourselves, however. God says that we are responsible for "setting free the mistreated" (Isaiah 58:6). We have a responsibility to take action to bring freedom to those who are oppressed.

Think about ways that you are responsible to others both locally and globally. How do your decisions and actions affect others in your neighborhood or town? In your state or our nation? In other parts of the world? How could you echo the Shout by taking action and fulfilling your responsibility to be part of setting free the oppressed? If you are reading this with a group of people, speak aloud places where freedom is needed: perhaps it is freedom from police brutality, or fear, or domestic violence, or addiction, or hunger, or something else that you might identify together. Determine what you can do together as a group to take action.

Art can be a source of freedom. It can set at liberty what is in our hearts and minds. It can provide an outlet for action to the timid, or it can set free the tortured spirit by creating space for truth to be proclaimed. Shout poet Gerald Cedillo has some thoughts on the importance of his art, poetry, in his fight for freedom:

Counter intuitive as it may seem, freedom is at once a center-stage spotlight and an empty clearing. It is equal parts megaphone and private writing. Whether they do so publicly or privately, whether they make it into art or none at all, artists try to delve into themselves and mine their mental and emotional states. The condition of being free, then, is determined by the access and accuracy we have to what is most authentic in us: our emotional selves. Poetry is how we bridge that far-off world of our thoughts and emotions with the stark reality of our day-to-day lives. Poetry provides a useful technique for remembering who we are, what we've done, how far we have progressed, and it brings out and emphasizes whatever repressive elements we face in ourselves and each other.

We speak of love having to be a verb; so freedom, too, must be performed. Freedom should be given melody and cadence and language, image and statement and metaphor.

Poetry is the most widely, most commonly accessible free press, an investigative journalism of the self. It contains the "news" of which William Carlos Williams emphasized "men die miserably every day for lack of what is found there" (From "Asphodel, That Greeny Flower," in *Journey to Love*; Random House, 1955). Poetry is the search for authenticity—all art should be, if we are to be honest—a technique with which we scrutinize our lives.

As we learn better the tools of scrutiny, these techniques open themselves to more possibilities, more use, and more power. Illuminating the difficult and formless experiences of our lives creates a set of knowledge, and with knowledge, responsibility, and with responsibility, action. To quote Audre Lorde: "That distillation of experience from which true poetry springs births thought as dream births concept, as feeling births idea, as knowledge births (precedes) understanding" (From "Poetry is Not a Luxury," in *Sister Outsider: Essays and Speeches*, by Audre Lorde; Crossing Press, 1984).

Art requires method, not just intuition. It requires a rigor to it, not just love. When we make art, when we write poetry, we are subjects to our inner-reality, but we must also be aware of the outer-reality to which this bridge takes us: the public, an audience. There must be controls in place for understanding, for entertainment, for acceptance.

MIKE COLLINS

Mike Collins is a homegrown Houstonian whose love is fantasy comic illustration. He taught himself to draw at age thirteen, and at fifty is still at it—more than forty years of honing his talent. He has done work for fundraisers and posters, and he is currently working on two graphic novels: *Genesis XIX* and *Nine*, a journey into a futuristic world gone nightmarishly mad.

There is an intellectual responsibility then to speak truthfully. Again, it is a responsibility to find and extract some authentic feeling or thought and present it to the world. In this way, poetry requires a great deal of cunning, the way one plans to commit a crime. One must commit a poem: to pledge oneself to a position on an issue or question; to carry it out, put it into effect, to execute it.

Here's a quote I think about often, from the ancient haiku master Matsuo Basho, as told by Robert Hass: "If the horror of the world were the truth of the world there would be no one to say it and no one to say it to." What could be more authentic in us than anger, pain, fear, the isolation that predominates so much romantic poetry? The same is true of joy, love, beauty. Freedom of speech, I heard someone once say, should be speech that makes others free and, as the philosophers tell us, man is no more himself than when at play. Poetry is meant to witness, to record, and from this duty we cannot shirk, but it is also meant to celebrate. This is also authentically us.

> The freedom within us should create freedom around us.

In Gerald's perspective, poetry is the battle for the truth to come out. There can be no communal truth without personal truth, and vice versa. The desire for holiness within us should reveal itself in a striving for holiness around us. The justice within us should create

65

justice around us. The freedom within us should create freedom around us. Yet we can only do that if we are brave enough to let the truth within us come out.

What truth do you need to set free? How might you do that? There are many avenues to release truth into the world: poetry, prose, dance, speech, music, or drawing can all be paths for the truth to become known. There are many others. Find out how to open the door to your soul, the opening through which your truth might help set others free. If you do not know already, then try some new things. Take that conversation that you had earlier about what area you needed to bring attention to as a group, and talk about how you could use your different skills to do so.

WHO DESERVES OUR RESPECT?

"Isn't it…covering the naked when you see them?" (Isaiah 58:7)

Recently, while driving, I was stopped at a red light by a man who was flying a sign. "Flying a sign" is slang for standing at an intersection and asking drivers for money. Moments like this always leave me feeling a bit conflicted. The light only permits seconds to have an interaction with the person at the intersection. As people hold signs ranging from the tragic to the humorous, it is easy in those instances simply to look away. I won't deny that I have often done so. Yet two of the men that I live in community with, who are among my closest friends, spent many years of their lives "flying a sign." Since I learned that, it has become impossible for me to look away. I cannot help but wonder about the lives of those I pass. I cannot help but feel a sense of warmth and love knowing that men so close to me also spent much of their lives in that manner. Relationship changes things. It may not always change my response, but it does change my mannerisms. It leads to a feeling of respect and intimacy where there was once a sense of division and distance.

Can you think of a time when a relationship changed the way that you viewed a person or people group? What are some of the ways that you were convicted and that your heart changed as a result?

Draw a picture that represents the impact that person or people had on you and how you changed.

When the gentleman stopped me at the red light, on that sunny afternoon on my way back into Houston from the Waller County Jail where I'd been sitting vigil, he caught me off guard. Instead of requesting money I had expected, the man said, "I'd rather have your hat than your money, ma'am." I couldn't help but smile. I knew the worth of the hat was $27.50, because I had lost it once before and had to buy a new one. Yet, locking eyes, both of us knew that the price of the hat had nothing to do with the transaction. There was something about the letters on the hat, PVAMU, standing for Prairie View A&M University, that meant something to him. I could tell. With a swift motion, I whipped the hat off my head with a chuckle and handed it out the window to him, saying, "Here you go, friend." His eyes lit up with surprise and delight. He cradled it in his hands as I drove away, both of us encouraged by the respect in our exchange.

Isaiah 58 describes the fast that God desires, and part of the prophet's vision for justice is "covering the naked when you see them" (Isaiah 58:7). It is simple on one level: There are people who lack adequate clothing, and God calls us to give them clothes. This is why clothing others has always been a foundational part of the Wesleyan movement. Back in the 1700's, when John Wesley and his friends were students at Oxford, they wanted to make

> People have, we realized, an even more foundational need than clothes: respect for their humanity.

the Christian faith a deeper part of their lives. They took a rigidly methodical approach to the faith. Other students mocked them as being "methodists." The name stuck, and John Wesley is regarded as the founder of Methodism. Along with Scripture study, holy conversation, and the sacraments, Wesley and his friends took it upon themselves to visit the poor and imprisoned, providing them with clothing and other necessities. It seems they strived to take seriously Jesus' words in Matthew 25: "I was hungry and you gave me food to eat. I was thirsty and you gave me a drink. I was a stranger and you welcomed me. I was naked and you gave me clothes to wear. I was sick and you took care of me. I was in prison and you visited me" (Matthew 25:35-36). Collecting clothes for those in need was one of the methods, or actions, that earned the first "methodists" their nickname.

Wesley and his fellow "methodists" fulfilled the Scriptures in a direct, concrete way: They literally clothed the naked, or the under-clothed. But when we discussed this line of Isaiah 58 as an open group at the Whisper, we saw "clothing the naked" pointing to something deeper. People have, we realized, an even more foundational need than clothes: respect for their humanity. That is what clothing represents: respect for one's humanity, dignity, and honor. Wesley and his friends clothed and visited the poor because they respected them, regarding them as human and valuing them as children of God.

After his days on the ark, the Scriptures tell us that Noah became drunk from some wine that he had made. His youngest son discovered him passed out naked in his tent. He went out and told his two brothers about it, and the older brothers did their best to preserve their father's dignity by covering him up:

"He drank some of the wine, became drunk, and took off his clothes in his tent. Ham, Canaan's father, saw his father naked and told his two brothers who were outside. Shem and Japheth took a robe, threw it over their shoulders, walked backward, and covered their naked father without looking at him because they turned away. When Noah woke up from his wine, he discovered what his youngest son had done to him" (Genesis 9:21-24).

Ham looked on Noah and seems to have mocked him, calling his older brothers to come and look. But Shem and Japheth covered their father, going to great lengths to do so without looking upon his naked body. The Scriptures make it clear that the different reactions of the sons revealed their character. The youngest son Ham did not respect his father, while the older two did. This is why Noah responds by cursing Ham's descendants, while blessing the older sons Shem and Japheth (Genesis 9:25-27). Whether or not we cover the naked has to do more with our character and our respect for others than it has to do with the other person. The greater shame is not in vulnerability, but in our derision of the vulnerability of others.

Who Deserves Our Respect?

When we asked "Who Deserves Our Respect?" at The Shout, it seemed to many to be a rhetorical question. "Everyone" seemed to be the obvious answer. But we soon discovered a deeper level to the question. If we say that everyone deserves our respect, do our actions and attitudes bear that out? In other words: Do we live as if this is true?

> The greater shame is not in vulnerability, but in our derision of the vulnerability of others.

Let's think for a minute about respect. In Aretha Franklin's beloved song, she sings, "R.E.S.P.E.C.T. Find out what it means to me." What does respect mean to you?

Write ten words that come to mind for you when you think about respect. Or consider the word "honor" if that is easier for you. Take those ten words and write a poem using them.

Go with whatever direction your heart takes you. Perhaps you feel led to write a confession for ways you have not shown respect to the vulnerable, or maybe you choose to celebrate someone who often goes unnoticed in your community. Or maybe you wish to give voice to the emotions or thoughts that accompany a feeling of respect, or a lack of it. There is no wrong way to respond. The goal is to help you uncover and explore what respect means for you.

Our society in general does not honor the vulnerable in ways that would please God. We find many veterans living on the streets instead of receiving care, love, and honor, and we typically respond by looking away or hurrying past. Our elderly often feel abandoned rather than being a part of our daily lives, and we don't call. Refugees and immigrants fleeing from violence that we have had a hand in creating are treated like criminals, even when they are children.

In 2015, there was a trial in Oklahoma for a police officer who was accused of raping thirteen African American women of the course of a few years (*www.cnn.com/2015/12/11/us/oklahoma-daniel-holtzclaw-verdict/*). Several of the women said that they didn't come forward because they did not think anyone would believe them. That says something about our society, about the way we treat those made vulnerable through sexism and racism. These women did not expect to be respected by those in power in their community or by the general public.

Often a lack of respect manifests itself as a silencing of voices. Draw a map of your community. Or better yet, if you have time, take a prayer walk around your community and take notes. Look for signs of disrespect. What do you notice? Is there any place where voices are being silenced? Perhaps the nursing home down the street. Perhaps the bridge where some homeless neighbors sleep at night. Perhaps the jail where people feel like they have been forgotten. Perhaps in homes with no visitors.

The SHOUT

In the space below, brainstorm about what you could do to help these voices to be heard. If you are in a group, do this as a group exercise and record your ideas. How could you work with your community not only to clothe the vulnerable, but to *hear* the vulnerable?

GERALD CEDILLO

Gerald Cedillo is from Houston, attended the University of St. Thomas, and studied creative writing at the University of Houston. He has taught theater, performance poetry, and writing. He is a literary event organizer and is on the board of Houston's week-long poetry festival, The Word Around Town.

Listen to the poem by Gerald Cedillo. Who does this poet respect? Why?

How does his response to the question, "Who deserves our respect?" challenge you?

Sometimes the best way to show respect to someone is simply to listen. Actually, that is always the best way to show respect. Often, when we want to make a change, our first impulse is to talk instead of listen; to tell instead of hear; to instruct instead of receive. We think we can figure out a solution to other people's problems without first listening to what they themselves think the problems in the world are. It brings to mind the Scripture that says we must remove the plank from our own eye before removing the speck from another's eye (Matthew 7:3-5). By telling someone how to fix their problems, we are telling them what we think is wrong with them or with their life. They may not agree.

> "Lord, to those who hunger, give bread. And to those who have bread, give a hunger for justice."—Latin American prayer

This is why a lot of young people have begun to discuss the dilemma of respectability politics in our culture. Respectability politics sounds like it is about respect, but it is actually about disrespect. In truth, it is not about respecting who a person is; it is about telling them who they should be. It is about imposing your standards onto someone else. It is about telling a person how you think they should act, dress, or talk in order to be respected. It means that you make certain demands of a person before you will offer them respect. For instance, one might say, "I'll treat you like you deserve respect when you treat yourself like you deserve respect and pull your pants up." It begins with *telling* rather than with *listening*.

Think of a time when you felt that people were treating you like you did not measure up. Make a list of things people have demanded of you in order to be worthy of respect.

If you feel led, draw a picture of how you see yourself and how others see you. Then take a black marker and cover up all the ways they wanted you to change. Now write the words: I am loved.

Read the following words from Psalm 8:5: "You've made them only slightly less than divine, crowning them with glory and grandeur." Feel in these words God's respect for you just as you are. Whether you are alone or in a group, pray a prayer of healing together for all the words, looks, and actions that have tried to diminish you.

The issue of respectability politics has become truly critical over the past couple of years as citizens in the United States have grappled with the disproportionate treatment of people of color by law enforcement. Often when a life is lost and people begin to hashtag a name, the same debate rises up immediately. On the one side you have those who feel that the solution to the profiling of people of color is to evaluate and change our policy and training, working intentionally to end systematic racism. On the other side there are those who respond that what's needed is training for young people of color, so that they will know how to interact with law enforcement. People on this side of the debate say that if Trayvon had not been wearing a hoodie, he would not have been stalked and shot; or if Eric had not been selling cigarettes, he would not have been choked on the street; or if Walter or Larry had not run away, they would not have been shot in the back; or if Rekia had not been standing in that neighborhood, she would not have been shot; or if Sandra had not insisted on knowing why she was being pulled from her car, she would not have found herself with her face down in the dirt and an officer's knee in her back while she yelled in pain.

> "You've made them only slightly less than divine, crowning them with glory and grandeur."

This is a very difficult conversation, and people on both sides have extreme emotions about it. You may feel powerful emotions now as you read and think about the issue, or it may spark intense debate within your group. This is a good place to pause and breathe. Take ten deep breaths. Perhaps try this rhythm of praying as you breath:

> Breathe in with these words in mind:
> Be still
> Breathe out: and know
> Breathe in: that I
> Breathe out: am God.

JEREMYAH "THE FLUENT ONE" PAYNE

Jeremyah "The Fluent One" Payne is one of the most renowned slam poets on the scene in Texas. The son of an AME pastor, Jeremyah studied computer science at Prairie View A&M University where he competed and toured with the Prairie View Productive Poets. After graduating, Jeremyah continued to compete with the Houston VIP team and competed as an individual to win the 2014 Texas Grand Slam Champion title. When he is not writing or producing videos, Jeremyah works as Senior Software Engineer at NASA in Houston, Texas.

Listen to the poem by Corinna Delgado. What vision of respect does she lift up? How does she challenge or encourage you?

Perhaps you are starting to see why the question of "Who Deserves Our Respect?" is not quite as rhetorical as people believed when they first heard it. It is easy to say that everyone deserves our respect, but it is harder to live that way, and as the saying goes, "Actions speak louder than words." We can say that the answer is simple, that everyone deserves our respect. Yet, when we turn away from suffering refugees, blame people for their own deaths, leave our elderly for months without a phone call or a visit, and refuse to make eye contact with the homeless neighbors on our streets, we give a different answer with our actions.

If we believe that all people are people of sacred worth, cherished by their creator, we cannot put the responsibility on the other to be 'worthy' of respect.

"Be still and know that I am God."

The SHOUT

TIFFANY "THE WORDMATICIAN" SCALES

Tiffany "The Wordmatician" Scales, known to some as Lyrik, is a poet with a talent unlike any other. Spitting lines off the top of her head, she feels the mood and needs of the room and brings healing to her listeners. Though born in Alabama, Tiffany has lived in Texas for twenty years and infuses elements of both states into her love for cooking. She is a proud graduate of Texas Southern University, where she studied Entertainment and Recording Management. An artist, activist, and advocate, Tiffany is the founder of Toiletries for Families, a non-profit that provides much-needed supplies so that struggling families do not have to choose between food and hygiene.

At The Shout, many poets responded to the question, "Who deserves our respect?" Tiffany "The Wordmatician" Scales gave such a powerful answer to this question, and I think we should close this period of reading with her words so that we can enter a space of prayer and contemplation:

At first I thought I would give all of my respect to Tom because he is the exception to the rule. He sleeps under the freeway, and walks to work...a job he was offered because he was spending most nights there anyway...he's deserving of my respect because he hasn't given up. I respect that.

Then, the list continued...

I also respect

1. The epitome of homelessness—those who exude the very image we have laid on them: tattered clothes, weary eyes, lines from smiles at passersby... wishing them a blessed day only hoping we could get a taste of what they would throw away.

2. Homeless veterans, partial (wo)men who fought for us to have legs to stand while they are in wheelchairs...judged for being drunk as though we could stand the nightmares.
   Sometimes I forget that I share their stories in a sense—fighting for something I believe to be worth it... only to fall back feeling worthless—not really understanding the point of it all until I've gotten to the point of exhaustion and there's still a breath in me... still energy left... Still an opportunity for me to confess—if I had it to do all over, I would do it again. The other day a young lady reminded me that I am NOT a black woman and moments after I was

reminded by another I was not white and I have to admit I've got a great deal of respect for

3. those who get through their day without crying and being angry because their features confuse others…For not hating themselves because others refuse to accept their complexion is their biggest complex.

The point is…we are deserving of respect. For our strength to do what others can't…won't. I'm not sure how to make it pretty when there's so much ugly to the truth…but I reckon that's the beauty of it all.

The way our differences are so similar. Take me for instance.

I'm not homeless either…not like you're used to…you know tattered clothes weary eyes or lines for passersby praying they have a blessed day because the lines are more so in my hand from being out stretched and closed again and outstretched and closed again trying to find out why nothing comes in them when I grasp when I clench but then I am reminded at red lights under overpasses when those headlights grow dim few and far between and sleep can come I remember the moment I laid in a hospital bed the same distractions kept me from peace it makes me think that all of us have walked the walk just to give ourselves the perception for the reality to be clear and even still we fall short.

In short, who deserves my respect? We do.

HOW MUCH IS ENOUGH?

"Isn't it sharing your bread with the hungry?" (Isaiah 58:7)

One of my favorite things about the Scriptures is that you can read them over and over again throughout your life and never stop discovering new ways to look at things. Part of this is because they are a living text. The Scriptures are living in the sense that the Spirit interacts with us in our reading and understanding. And they are living in the sense that there is always a constantly expanding community that interprets and brings new perspectives and experiences to the text. For instance, the first time I heard the story of Mary's pregnancy with Jesus preached by a woman, I immediately felt excitement. I also felt sadness for all those many generations, all those hundreds of years that people had never gotten to hear the text preached by someone who had actually felt the pain, and danger, and mess of childbirth for herself. All those years we did not let women in our pulpits. What a loss.

There are so many ways to understand our living text more deeply, and we need each other—we need to hear as much of the community as possible—in order to understand the Scriptures as well as we can. For instance, how can we understand Isaiah 58:7, "Isn't it sharing your bread with the hungry," if we had never been hungry? What if all that hunger means to us is that we are late for supper?

If we have never heard the story of Jesus' birth preached by a woman who has given birth, we are missing out on something. In the same way, if we have never heard about hunger from someone for whom it could mean death, we are missing out on something. We cannot truly understand what the Scriptures are calling us to do. In both cases, what we are missing out in large part is *danger*.

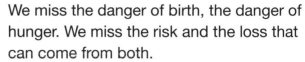

We miss the danger of birth, the danger of hunger. We miss the risk and the loss that can come from both.

In the case of the latter, hunger, the Scriptures are calling us to do something about it: When you see the hungry, feed them. If someone is hungry, that indicates a need. If you are able to feed them, that indicates a surplus.

How can we understand Isaiah if we have never been hungry?

In other words, that exhortation from Isaiah communicates three things. First, it communicates that there are some who are in need of food, some who are hungry. Second, it communicates that there are some who have a surplus of food, enough food that they can share. Third, it communicates that those who have more should give to those who have less.

Which brings us to our question: How much is enough? Knowing how much is enough helps us to identify what our "more than enough" is. This is important because when we know what our "more than enough" is, we know what has been given to us so that we might give it to others.

I'm assuming that if you have access to this book, you are not in a place where you have to choose between eating and reading. But maybe you have been in that place at one point. Or maybe I'm wrong in my assumption, and you did have to sacrifice a meal or two in order to read these words. Or maybe you have been hungry for something apart from food. Without distracting from or diminishing the importance of addressing physical hunger in our world, we also need to account for other needs that are just as real.

What are some areas where you have experienced need or hunger? If you are able, draw an image that represents that need.

The SHOUT

When you were in a place of need, were there others who were able to meet that need? Did they choose to do so, or not? How did that make you feel? Make a list of five words, either positive or negative (or both), that describe that experience for you. Share you responses with the other members of your group if you are reading this book in a group setting.

Among all the spoken word artists that we find in the Scriptures, the artists who best express what need feels like are actually the lyricists of the Psalms. The heart-wrenching outcry of need and the gratitude that comes when that need is met are found in the words of the Psalms. Rather than a summons to action for us, they are often a request for action from God. They remind us that there are some needs that no person can meet. They remind us that it is okay to be honest with God when we reach the end of what we can endure.

Read Psalms 44, 142, and 73, which are printed on the following pages. Are there any you identify with? How so?

Psalm 44

1 We have heard it, God, with our own ears;
    our ancestors told us about it:
        about the deeds you did in their days,
        in days long past.
2 You, by your own hand, removed all the nations,
        but you planted our ancestors.
    You crushed all the peoples,
        but you set our ancestors free.
3 No, not by their own swords
    did they take possession of the land—
        their own arms didn't save them.
    No, it was your strong hand, your arm,
    and the light of your face
        because you were pleased with them.
4 It's you, God! You who are my king,
    the one who orders salvation for Jacob.
5 We've pushed our foes away by your help;
    we've trampled our enemies by your name.
6 No, I won't trust in my bow;
    my sword won't save me

7   because it's you who saved us from our foes,
    you who put those who hate us to shame.

8 So we glory in God at all times
    and give thanks to your name forever. Selah

9 But now you've rejected and humiliated us.
    You no longer accompany our armies.

10 You make us retreat from the enemy;
    our adversaries plunder us.

11 You've handed us over like sheep for butchering;
    you've scattered us among the nations.

12 You've sold your people for nothing,
    not even bothering to set a decent price.

13 You've made us a joke to all our neighbors;
    we're mocked and ridiculed by everyone around us.

14 You've made us a bad joke to the nations,
    something to be laughed at by all peoples.

15 All day long my disgrace confronts me,
    and shame covers my face

16   because of the voices of those
    who make fun of me and bad-mouth me,
      because of the enemy who is out for revenge.

17 All this has come upon us,
    but we haven't forgotten you
    or broken your covenant.

18 Our hearts haven't turned away,
    neither have our steps strayed from your way.

19 But you've crushed us in the place where jackals live,
    covering us with deepest darkness.

20 If we had forgotten the name of our God

or spread out our hands to some strange deity,
21 wouldn't God have discovered it?

After all, God knows every secret of the heart.
22 No, God, it's because of you that we are
getting killed every day—

it's because of you that we are considered
sheep ready for slaughter.
23 Wake up! Why are you sleeping, Lord?

Get up! Don't reject us forever!
24 Why are you hiding your face,

forgetting our suffering and oppression?
25 Look: we're going down to the dust;

our stomachs are flat on the ground!
26 Stand up! Help us!

Save us for the sake of your faithful love.

Psalm 142

1 I cry out loud for help from the LORD.

I beg out loud for mercy from the LORD.
2 I pour out my concerns before God;

I announce my distress to him.
3 When my spirit is weak inside me, you still
know my way.

But they've hidden a trap for me in the path I'm
taking.
4 Look right beside me: See?

No one pays attention to me.
There's no escape for me.

No one cares about my life.
5 I cry to you, LORD, for help.

"You are my refuge," I say.

"You are all I have in the land of the living."

⁶ Pay close attention to my shouting,
  because I've been brought down so low!
Deliver me from my oppressors
  because they're stronger than me.
⁷ Get me out of this prison
  so I can give thanks to your name.
Then the righteous will gather all around me
  because of your good deeds to me.

Psalm 73

¹ Truly God is good to Israel,
  to those who are have a pure heart.
² But me? My feet had almost stumbled;
  my steps had nearly slipped
³   because I envied the arrogant;
  I observed how the wicked are well off:
⁴ They suffer no pain;
  their bodies are fit and strong.
⁵ They are never in trouble;
  they aren't weighed down like other people.
⁶ That's why they wear arrogance like a necklace,
  why violence covers them like clothes.
⁷ Their eyes bulge out from eating so well;
  their hearts overflow with delusions.
⁸ They scoff and talk so cruel;
  from their privileged positions
  they plan oppression.
⁹ Their mouths dare to speak against heaven!
  Their tongues roam the earth!
¹⁰ That's why people keep going back to them,
  keep approving what they say.
¹¹ And what they say is this: "How could God

possibly know!

    Does the Most High know anything at all!"

[12] Look at these wicked ones,

    always relaxed, piling up the wealth!

[13] Meanwhile, I've kept my heart pure for no good reason;

I've washed my hands to stay innocent for nothing.

[14] I'm weighed down all day long.

    I'm punished every morning.

[15] If I said, "I will talk about all this,"

    I would have been unfaithful to your children.

[16] But when I tried to understand these things,

    it just seemed like hard work

[17]   until I entered God's sanctuary

      and understood what would happen to the wicked.

[18] You will definitely put them on a slippery path;

    you will make them fall into ruin!

[19] How quickly they are devastated,

    utterly destroyed by terrors!

[20] As quickly as a dream departs from someone waking up, my Lord,

    when you are stirred up, you make them disappear.

[21] When my heart was bitter,

    when I was all cut up inside,

[22] I was stupid and ignorant.

    I acted like nothing but an animal toward you.

[23] But I was still always with you!

    You held my strong hand!

[24] You have guided me with your advice;

    later you will receive me with glory.

25 Do I have anyone else in heaven?
  There's nothing on earth I desire except you.
26 My body and my heart fail,
  but God is my heart's rock and my share
forever.
27 Look! Those far from you die;
  you annihilate all those who are unfaithful to
you.
28 But me? It's good for me to be near God.
  I have taken my refuge in you, my Lord God,
    so I can talk all about your works!

Do the lyrics in these Psalms remind you of any song lyrics you have heard? Often musicians help express emotion best. What music have you heard that echoes need?

It is important for us to remember that there are some needs we cannot meet for one another; there are some needs that only God can meet. When we try to meet all the needs of others or seek for others to meet all our needs, we can find ourselves empty.

JASMINNE MENDEZ

Jasminne Mendez is an award-winning author, poet, educator, and spoken-word artist who wants to share her experiences with you and the world. She has been published both nationally and internationally, and her book *Island of Dreams* was published in 2013. Jasminne believes in the power of words and whole-heartedly accepts that art can save lives. Check out her website, *www.jasminnemendez.com*, which is dedicated to promoting her work, sharing and booking upcoming performances and appearances, and creating a space where writers young and old can connect and grow as a community.

In Jasminne Mendez's poem, she spoke about seeking to do the best she could and still knowing that it would not be enough.

What is a need that you have that no human could ever be enough to fulfill? Looking at some of the Psalms above, write your own Psalm to answer this question. Do not feel like you have to make it fit the language of the past. Use the words that feel natural to you, the rhythm that feels natural to you. Make it a modern Psalm that is authentic to who you are. Be playful and try to create something new.

It is important not to look to others in desperation for something that only God can provide. At the same time, however, that does not excuse us from doing all we can to meet the needs of those whom we are able to help and who are counting on us. Isaiah is clear that God expects us to share our bread with the hungry; those of us who have "more than enough" must share with those who have "not enough," so that all may truly have enough.

If you are more of a mathematical, logical thinker and all of this artistic exploration has been not quite your speed, this, my friend, is the moment you have been waiting for in this conversation. This is your moment to shine.

Help your friends understand this equation:

$$(X+5) + (X-5) = X$$

Now replace X with "enough" and the plus 5 or minus 5 with "more" or "less."

(More than enough) + (Not enough) = Enough

Think about a time when you had a physical need and that need was met. Even if you prayed for it and you felt God answered you, the thing you needed probably did not come down in a parachute drop from heaven. It is most likely that some human being played role in meeting that need. God acts to meet our needs, but God most often acts through other people to do so.

Time for more math. Here is another equation that we might consider:

(Prayer to God) + (Action by faithful) = Need met

Now that we have delighted our math lovers and horrified the math averse, let's return to the conversation at hand.

Do you remember the reflection from Nyne in Chapter 2 based on the question, "Who Is Your Family?" (pages 47–48)? In his way of looking at things, part of how he knew someone was truly family was how they responded if he was in trouble or in need. They were there for him to do what they could to help. One example he used was bailing a friend out of jail. Another example he used was when a friend helped him get home when he lost his wallet. Both of these examples involve a financial sacrifice of some kind. While we can get really awkward and uncomfortable when talking about money, the truth is: It matters. How we use our resources, including money, matters to the people around us. That's what Isaiah meant by saying, "Isn't it sharing your bread with the hungry?"

We can say we are family all day and all night, but when someone close to us has that crucial "less than enough" and we have "more than enough" and we do not come to their aid, it certainly has an impact. When we do come to their aid, that has an impact too. This is not to say we are to be without boundaries and discernment. We do need to have "enough" spiritually, physically, and financially, or it will put all of us in a bad position. There is a big piece in this for spiritual discernment, and an even bigger piece for conviction. But when we do have more than enough, God calls us to share it.

To put it bluntly, for some of us to have enough, others of us will have to have less. That is simply the way the math works.

This causes fear for some, a mindset dominated by scarcity in which people are afraid that they will be the ones who will not have enough. This fear leads them to actions that protect what they have, and sometimes hoard what they have, resulting in others truly having less.

JAMES "ROOSTER" TROTTER

James Trotter is an award-winning writer, humorist, musician, slam poet, actor, and educator, and he is a founding member of the hiphop improv theatre The Space Rhyme Continuum. He has performed live all over the United States as well as in Europe and Asia. James's work has garnered critical praise, with ThreeWiseMonkeys.com heralding his "surreal, irreverent humor." He facilitates a creative writing workshop for the homeless through Servants of Christ United Methodist Church, and he teaches the art of writing and performance through the nonprofit organization Writers in the Schools.

In the group poem by Outspoken Bean, Nyne, The Fluent One, and Rooster, they spoke about this issue. How does their performance address fear? What specific actions does it speak out against, and how do those actions reflect a mindset of scarcity?

Write your reaction to their poem and the circumstances they speak of below.

"The alternative to a mindset of scarcity is a mindset of abundance, where we trust that there will be enough for all."

The alternative to a mindset of scarcity is a mindset of abundance, where we trust that there will be enough for all. This is what we are called to cultivate in our lives, because God does provide enough for all. Yet it requires some responsibility on our part. It requires some awareness, some honesty with ourselves of how the "enough" is distributed and how we have "more than enough." When we are not honest with ourselves about the fact that we have more than enough, we will slip back into an attitude of scarcity in order to protect ourselves.

Take a handful of rice, beans, sand, or beads...be creative, the exact object doesn't matter as long as it's something that can flow. Grab a handful of it in your left hand. Now try to pass it back and forth between your hands until you have an equal amount in each hand. The hand on the left has less than what it started with, but that is because it chose to open up and release what it had so that the other hand would not be empty.

That is the reality that we actually face a lot of the time in this world. It's not simply that one hand has a little more than the other and it just is "not fair." Rather, one of the hands is truly empty. While some people feel well protected, others feel that there is nowhere where they are safe. While some people feel well fed, others feel their life expiring for lack of sustenance. The question

is not whether solving this problem is good politics, good policy, good patriotism, or good economics. The question is whether it is good character, good faithfulness, good discipline, and good compassion.

This is not the way most people choose to live. Honestly admitting that we have "more than enough" and then giving away our surplus goes against the grain. It is difficult, which means it will involve sacrifice. And that is what makes it so very necessary that you choose to live in this way. Because while some of us feast, others of us starve. While some of us breathe free, others gasp for air. I don't write this to make you you feel guilty if you are the one with the "more than enough" money, or food, or safety, or air. Do not for a second let yourself slip into shame, for shame immobilizes us. Reject guilt and shame, and claim conviction and responsibility. Once we know, we have the ability and responsibility to act. Once we understand, we have the ability and responsibility to teach. How much is enough? Answer that question, and then share your surplus.

"While some of us feast, others of us starve."

CORINNA DELGADO

Born and raised in Anchorage, Alaska, Corinna Delgado is a first-generation Japanese American. Delgado is a performance poet, public speaker, published author, visual artist, journalist, and broadcaster. She has written for *The Anchorage Daily News*, *The Anchorage Press*, and *The Northern Light*. With two poetry collections and a writing workbook published under her indie publishing label, RockFish Indie Press, Delgado is set to release her first art book this spring. Delgado was previously a reporter and anchor for Fox & ABC affiliates in Alaska, but her primary role in broadcast has been as a radio personality. She is presently on air with 94.7 KZND in Anchorage, Alaska and on 104.1 KRBE in Houston. Find more information at Corinna-Delgado.com

There will be moments that come when there is nothing that we can do. We will not have what another person needs. For those moments, poet Corinna Delgado wrote this modern Psalm herself for when our presence is all that we can give, and for the moment, it will have to be enough.

Soldier Song for the Suffocated
I set forth to write a song for you
Something that would see you through; keep faith afoot and
perseverance in your lungs
…and when you'd exhale during the difficult part of your journey
Your labored breath would sound like hope
And song.

I dug deep … to the natural rhythm of my feet, and the sway in my
_   hip_
I looked for song in the nod of my head and the purse of my lips
Lyrics licked / like envelopes
I had hoped
To recount my own downward slopes and find the fuel
And tools
Necessary to compose your song …

but I've been singing too long.
hymnals … spirituals … and heart break anthems;
A triathlon of songs - pantin'
"I will survive" and "lord I'm coming "–
the repetitive humming Creates a familiar buzz
no more noticeable than the whiiiiirrrrrrr of our computers.
_   Whereas; once_
A song

*Could inspire nations to part seas, virgins to part knees, and the
    suffocated to breathe
But if you have been singing for survival every mile of the way
The melody starts to lose its taste*

*The over chewed cud – of we shall overcome … begins to wear
    away at the tongue
I've sung
So many songs of survival
That my recant would nothing more than minimize your trial
My off key out of tune / is no redemption song for your doom
And soon
I started to feel that singing you lovely lullabies
Was a far cry / from what you needed.*

*Composer defeated …
I whispered to myself "retreat"… and
somehow found no shame in it.*

*Once upon a time we were soldiers
And we were sold this
Idea that retreat was delayed defeat – and that rest was for the
    wicked – and a moment to cease…
And peace
Was only afforded to the weak.
Speak nothing wars and worlds of warriors and "rest"… in the
    same breath*

*Slave masters and over lords spun such webs … and we
We tricked our souls with songs of salvation
In order to fulfill unreal expectations.*

Servant
surf
gentile ... Jew
the disenfranchised, and every under privileged child too
we were taught to pull thru
thriving ...surviving our struggle with the sound of our song

but before we happily sing along
consider this
regarding the tyranny of the oppressed
in the game of chess
it is solely the pawn which is required to continually press
only forward.

There are no symphonies here.
No chorus that would trick the ear ... or harmony to harp the
    heart.
Notes as sharp as spears, fallacy of falsetto
Tenor of thy tears, allow your vibrato to settle

And silence your song.
Stop.
Breaaaaaathhhhhhe
and I will sing along in your silence to the chorus of only breathing
the notes...

And somehow
The exhale will still
Sound like hope.

Sit long enough in that space of another's pain, and it will
cease to be difficult to make the sacrifices we need to make

for all to have enough. It is relationship that summons forth responsibility. While guilt and shame drive a wedge in our relationships, sowing division rather than solidarity, presence and responsibility brings us closer together and closer to the place where all of us have enough.

HOW CAN WE BE WHOLE?

"Then your light will break out like the dawn, and you will be healed quickly" (Isaiah 58:8).

When the Scripture tells us that we will be healed quickly, the words are the words used to describe the new flesh that appears in a healing wound. We might imagine it as the first layer of skin that springs up to cover the injury as healing begins. If you have ever had what is commonly referred to as a boo-boo, however, you know that there is a lot more to the healing process than just that initial springing up of fresh skin. There are layers and layers of healing that will take place as your body returns to full strength and wholeness. THE SHOUT question, "How can we be whole?" asks about this healing process.

When the wound is within a community rather than to an individual body, the healing process, likewise, takes time, as well as truth and intentionality. That is why the whole passage of Isaiah 58, especially verses 6-7, is full of instructions for how to experience wholeness in our relationship with God and others, as well as within ourselves. Rather than a list of "don'ts," Isaiah presents his readers with a list of "dos."

It's as if each "do" adds a layer of healing to the community. Each aspect of a God-pleasing, justice-oriented fast draws into closer fellowship someone who has felt like he or she is on the outside. Each hungry person fed is one more person who has been made whole, which means the community itself has taken one more step toward wholeness. Each person who is covered, respected, and uplifted is one more whole person in the community, making the community a little bit healthier.

What wounds are there in your community? What healing needs to occur? Draw an image of what adding layers of healing would do within your community.

That is one of the keys to understanding why Isaiah 58 is such a powerful passage of Scripture. God approaches a people who are concerned with their own individual wholeness rather than the community's wholeness. They fast from food, but they quarrel (Isaiah 58:4). They fast from work, but they oppress their workers on the same day (58:3). They wear sackcloth and ashes instead of regular clothes, right after striking one another with angry fists (58:4-5). They are concerned with their personal advancement in the spiritual realm, behaving as if every sacrifice they make gains them points that help them get ahead with God.

Yet God wants the people to know that there is no getting ahead with God. Having a relationship with God is not a competition, and there can be no right relationship with God without being in a right relationship with others. A relationship with God is not to be sought in a way that does harm to others, creating wounds rather than remedies.

John Wesley said that there is no holiness but social holiness. In other words, it is not a personal affair. We cannot be holy individually with no authentic regard for the holiness of our community. In the same way, we cannot seek to be whole individually without pursuing the wholeness of our community. We cannot promote healing without being willing to be honest about what has caused the wound and seeking to end it.

"Let the preson who has ears, hear" (Mathew 11:15)

It is often the case that wounds go far deeper than we realize. Sometimes wounds are so deep that layers of dead or infected skin must be removed in order for healing to occur. Death must be removed for life to thrive. And certainly, the root cause of the wound must be dealt with. Healing that springs up quickly will soon be reversed if the same activity that caused the wound is still taking place.

Consider the social problem of racism, for instance. Sometimes in the struggle to end racism, people say that slavery is over or segregation is over, so the conversation should be finished. Such a viewpoint, however, fails to realize that slavery and segregation are the wound itself, not the cause of the wound. That new layer of skin that has sprung up quickly will be in danger if we continually rub that wound in the same manner that created it at the beginning. Slavery and formal segregation may have stopped, but racism will wound in other ways as long as it continues to exist. In order to be whole, in order to truly heal, repair, and restore, we also need to stop doing the behavior that created harm.

To use another analogy, slavery and segregation are symptoms of the disease, not the disease itself. If a person has a virus and we only clean up their mess and mop the sweat from their brow, we are addressing the symptoms but not the cause of their sickness. Often medication, rest, and hydration are necessary to end the illness. A vaccine or a change in environment might be needed in order to prevent the virus from recurring. If racism is the disease behind the symptoms, then we must end racism or it will simply continue to infect the body in different places and different manners.

If we are to be called Mender of Broken Walls and Restorer of Livable Streets (Isaiah 58:12), then healing must be about more than just allowing the layers of kindness and compassion and respect to increase. It must also be about confronting the things that have been creating wounds in our hearts, the breaches in our walls, the potholes in our streets. That work will take shape differently for different people, depending on whether they have been the ones wounded or the ones doing the wounding. The important thing is that we all begin to confront the cause of the wounds in our communities.

That type of work takes honesty and courage. Once we have fed the hungry, we have to ask ourselves why they were hungry in the first place. Once we have covered the naked, we must ask ourselves why they were looked on with scorn in the past. Once we have brought the homeless into our home, then we must enter into a relationship with them and begin to ask ourselves how our community can change so they do not find themselves in that situation again.

Jesus said, "Let the person who has ears, hear," an admonishment for his listeners to pay close attention to his words (Matthew 11:15). Often, that is the way the work of healing will look. Some people will have ears to hear and will want to engage in the work. Others will not and may even try to block the work that is needed.

Having ears to hear often means paying close, compassionate attention to the cries of others. Like a doctor, don't react to how the person's response to a wound makes you feel. Instead, react with compassion and a commitment to try to identify the source of the wound. For instance, a woman might say, "My voice as a woman is important!" She does not say this because men's voices are not important. It may be because she has been wounded by being told, either directly or subtly, that her voice did not matter. Perhaps she was told she could not speak from the pulpit at her church because she was a woman. Or perhaps she noticed that when she was at school, her peers laughed at her questions. Somewhere there is a wound behind her words.

Try to identify the wounds that created the necessity for the words printed below. Write or draw your response in the space provided.

BLACK LIVES MATTER

ALL MEANS

S

All means all

Black Lives Matter

Sí se puede

The SHOUT

Sometimes wounds are personal, the result of an individual being singled out for abuse or disrespect. Other times wounds are communal, the result of a group of people who are treated like they are less valuable because of their race, ethnicity, gender, orientation, language, or some other characteristic. We have to figure out the source of the wound and address it. Perhaps it lies in our friend group. Perhaps it lies in our government. Perhaps it lies in our own heart.

LUPE MENDEZ

Originally from Galveston, Texas, Lupe works with Nuestra Palabra: Latino Writers Having Their Say, the Word Around Poetry Tour, and the Brazilian Arts Foundation to promote poetry events, advocate for literacy/literature, and organize creative writing workshops that are open to the public. Mendez has over fifteen years of experience as a performance poet, having opened for such notable writers as Dagoberto Gilb, Oscar Casarez, Esmeralda Santiago, and the late Raul Salinas. Lupe is an internationally published poet in print and electronic mediums. Lupe's work reflects his roots in Texas and the Mexican state of Jalisco, and it comments on commonplace issues, struggles, moments, relevant ideas, and images he is humbled to witness.

The poem by Jeremyah Payne says that the opposite of fear is love. How can love give us the courage to be whole?

What are some of the layers of infection that need to be removed from our communal wounds in order for healing to begin? Draw a picture or write a poem if you prefer.

We ask how can *we* be whole instead of how can I be whole, because not one of us can be whole in isolation while people God loves are suffering around us. If we think we can, it is an illusion, and we have to be brave enough to confront it.

BLANCA ALANIS

Blanca Rodriguez Alanis is a mother, poet, and human rights activist. She's also a self-taught artesana and photographer. In 2008, she opened the first Spanish bilingual bookstore in Houston. Her first work was published by Boundless in 2010, The Rio Grande Valley International Poetry Festival. Her bilingual poetry book *Puro Corazon* was released in 2013. She has been a spoken-word performer and served as co-organizer for Houston's Word Around Town Poetry Tour. She has participated in the Annual Frida Festival, Women with Disability Empowerment Fair, and Houston's International Women's Festival.

One of the most powerful moments that ever happened at The Shout was when one of our poet activists, Blanca Alanis, arranged for a group to come and speak. The group was being hosted in town for the week by Alianza Mexicana, and they were called AMIREDIS, Asociación de Migrantes Retornados con Discapacidad (Association of Returned Migrants with Disabilities). They were on their way across the nation to share their story in Washington, DC. As the group of men came to the microphone, they barely needed translation to convey their point.

Each one of them was missing a limb from having survived The Beast.

The Beast, or *La Bestia*, refers to the trains on the freight network that runs the length of Mexico from Guatemala to the United States (see *www.npr.org/sections/ parallels/2014/06/05/318905712/riding-the-beast-across-mexico- to-the-u-s-border*). Though these aren't passenger trains, many people (including children) ride the train in hopes of crossing to the United States. Among other hardships, they face the risk of death or serious injury from falling off the train while it's moving. The Beast claims many lives.

Like gladiators, these men visiting The Shout marched on as if the loss of an arm here or a leg there could not stop them from triumph. As they ascended the few steps to the platform on prosthetic legs, their presence did not summon an ounce of pity because the respect they commanded in the room left space for no other emotion.

These are men who found conditions in their nation of origin to be so bad that they had climbed on board the top of a train to escape. Falling off, each one had become one of the many who attempted the risk and one of the few who survived a collision with a train. As the men finished speaking, Blanca shared a poem in their honor.

The moment was life changing for many in our community. For months, we had been holding Whispers at a social justice focused arts Museum in Houston called The Station Museum. They had an exhibit called Detention Nation, which was a simulation of a detention center bunk room with art and letters from children and adults who were still in detention on the walls. A deeper connection had begun to form when someone mentioned a troubling similarity between the immigrant detention industry and the prison industrial complex. Both had been shifting towards becoming for-profit industries.

> "We ask how can *we* be whole instead of how can I be whole, because not one of us can be whole in isolation while people God loves are suffering around us."

That may seem like an economic concern, not a spiritual concern. But in fact, it is a justice concern, and justice is often an economic concern and always a spiritual concern.

Take a minute to search out information about Judge Mark Ciavarella, Jr. and the "kids for cash" scandal. A judge in Pennsylvania, he was accused of receiving bribes to send young people to for-profit juvenile detention centers, and he was convicted on a number of charges in 2011.

The scandal rightly drew outrage from the community, especially from parents whose children had been imprisoned. When imprisonment becomes privately owned and for profit, and sometimes even when it is not, each body in a cell represents dollars paid to the institution to hold them. No bodies, no money. The bodies are necessary for the business to continue. What does wholeness mean for the people involved in this situation and others like it? What wounds exist, and what shape can healing take?

AUDREY OMENSON

Audrey is an artist based in Houston, Texas. She works primarily with acrylic, mixed media, and ink to create fine art, commissions, and live painting at events. She calls herself a "postmodern impressionist," blending classical art techniques with themes from psychology, theology, social justice, and even Euclidean geometry. In all of her art, her goal is to create beautiful, thought-provoking work that invites the viewer to step into something larger than their individual self and connect with the story of another. She is also a counselor at a local nonprofit and working towards a master of divinity through Fuller Theological Seminary.

As we know, the love of money is the root of all evil:

Actually, godliness is a great source of profit when it is combined with being happy with what you already have. We didn't bring anything into the world and so we can't take anything out of it: We'll be happy with food and clothing. But people who are trying to get rich fall into temptation. They are trapped by many stupid and harmful passions that plunge people into ruin and destruction. The love of money is the root of all kinds of evil. Some have wandered away from the faith and have impaled themselves with a lot of pain because they made money their goal. (1 Timothy 6:6-10)

When the men from AMIREDIS spoke to us at The Shout, we had all been aware of problems caused by the for-profit detention industry. But despite what we knew, there was something different about seeing in person what people were losing. To see their bodies, to hear their voices, to hear Blanca's poem—all of it was life changing because it cut to people's hearts.

When those men stepped onto the stage, missing arms and legs because of their journey for freedom, those who had struggled to feel compassion for the immigrants in our community finally felt their walls come down. The solidarity that had been building among us became concrete. It happened not simply because of some emotional response to that event, but because of all the Whispering we had done leading up to it: all of the hard work of education, conversations, and listening. But that night was a watershed moment for us. To know and see that people were willing to lose limbs, lose lives, in order to find freedom brought a whole new depth to the conversation.

When we understand that the question is not "How can I be whole?" but is "How can *we* be whole?" then we can start to understand that we must consider how our actions impact everyone around us.

The SHOUT

Few people can explain this so eloquently as The Fluent One, Jeremyah Payne. I leave you with his words, in the hope that you too may find a way to be whole. Hear the Shout, and then Echo it in your community.

In order for us to be whole we must first recognize that we are a collection of parts that have a profound effect on the others. While we are often taught our uniqueness and the identity of free will, it easy to overlook our impact we have in the entropic system we reside in.

In the United States we exist in a theory of bootstraps and opportunity, that on your own you can change the axis of the earth. It easy to overlook other people's struggle when you are aware of your own. To know first hand what you have overcome, while remaining ignorant of the daily fight of others.

What is beautifully more complicated are the varying levels of effort and tolerance, or even the balance between reception and intention. It is easy to say you should accept my action because of my good intention. It is harder to ignore your good intention and focus on the negative reception by others of your action.

To be whole, is not to discard either the intention or the reception. We must all strive to do better, to love better, to uplift, and to acknowledge each other as Christ did. Knowing how different the backgrounds of each disciple are we still refer to "them" as the "The Twelve", refer to the sons of Jacob as "The Tribe", as we should refer to ourselves as the "The Body" of Christ.

People have a tendency to justify their actions and beliefs. We do this with associations and perceptions of how we view ourselves. This goes all the way back to Cain and Abel, with Cain trying to justify his sacrifice. If we think of ourselves as good or well intentioned, then if we do something that is received otherwise it conflicts with our perception of ourselves. Some are able to take chastisement and learn, but for most of us it is difficult to adapt and continuously learn. The schism of our self perception and received perception can be confusing.

Stop looking at your reflection trying to cut out the parts of the mirror that make you look bad, you only end up with broken glass and bloody fingers. We will hold a false confidence that we are ready for more, bearing the weight of the world on cracked shoulders confusing the swaggered over limp for carrying a chip.

We don't understand. We children hiding under the covers when the lights go off, afraid of the boogey men and the gay men. Sure that whatever comes out of the closet is meant to harm us, wrapping their talons around our petrified ankles dragging us screaming under the bed

We fear what we don't understand because we fear not having control. It's a scary world, It's a balance of spontaneity and unpredictability. There are some who cannot understand NOT having control over their every decision and there are some that can't understand having control over ANY decision

It can be difficult to try to understand all that makes us different and unique. But I understand love, I understand support, I understand defending truth, I understand grey better than i ever did black and white, I understand we are kaleidoscope dreams even when the rules of the universe don't apply to the universe.

What math works down at the atomic level, does not translate to the galactic scale and yet, the universe exists. We are all paradoxes, part of an equation that does not exit yet we variables, we Xs and Ys each have our parts to live, to love, to build. It's a funny thing about us and gravity. That when you are 3/4 of a millimeter from someone, you exert just as much gravity on them as the sun. It's amazing, how we're all stars like that.

And that I understand.